The

GUERN

HANDBOOK©

2024 Edition

by
Tony Brassell

Lighthouse, St Peter Port, Guernsey

Cover Image: View of
Castle Cornet, Guernsey

Dedicated to my wonderful family.
Photos by Tony Brassell unless otherwise
credited.

ISBN - 9798876725035

Introduction

Guernsey is one of several Islands in the Bay of St Malo, easily accessible by air from many UK and European locations, including Gatwick and Southampton and by sea from South Coast ports and St Malo in France.

Once a popular location for a 2-week beach holiday, it has become increasingly popular as a short break destination for independent travelers, as well as being a regular stop for Cruise liners.

The Bailiwick of Guernsey is a group of Islands (under the control of a Bailiff), which includes Alderney, Sark and Herm. All are within sight of each other, which gives the location an almost tropical quality, with views across to the other Islands from all but the West Coast of Guernsey, which faces the Atlantic.

On a bright summer's day, the views from St Peter Port in Guernsey are some of the finest in the world.

St Peter Port has become a cosmopolitan town, full of fine restaurants and niche retail outlets, while remaining steeped in history and folklore.

In Guernsey, there is something for everyone. If you like walking along cliff paths or jumping into the sea from the bottom of the cliffs, you can do that.

If you like small boats, fishing or lazing on beaches, you can do that too. If cycling is for you or just exploring country lanes in the car – well, you know what I am going to say.

I have lived on the Island for more than 60 years and I still find new corners, new views, and new things to do all the time, so your break in Guernsey can easily be filled with activities if you want it to be.

However, if relaxing is your idea of heaven, Guernsey is one of the best places in the world to do that. The pace of life outside of St Peter Port is relaxed to say the least, with great hotels and restaurants ideally placed to make your visit truly wonderful. So, get out the paints, stroll the cliffs, take stunning photographs, lie on a beach, take a boat trip to another island and live your dreams.

I can guarantee you will never forget your visit to Guernsey and like many people before you, you might just keep coming back for more.

In the following pages I will set out all the information you will need to enjoy a wonderful holiday in the beautiful, British, Channel Island of Guernsey.

You may even want to move here.

If you do, visit – www.locateguernsey.com

I have lived in Guernsey for 66 years and like all residents of similar places we can easily take our homes for granted. But some days, when the sun is shining, the sea is flat calm, and everyone around you is smiling and says hi, you remember just how amazing Guernsey is, and how it might look to people who have never been here before.

Our son-in-law spends his summers operating Island Rib Voyages, a local boat cruise business. They provide sightseeing tours around the Islands coast. While our daughter runs Craftwise, the Islands only dedicated retail outlet dedicated to Crafting. They are based in Oatlands Village.

You might even find me behind the counter if you visit over a weekend.

From time to time, we get the opportunity to go out on an Island Rib tour and they are brilliant fun, the experience never dulls.

I have seen places I had never seen before, watched Atlantic Grey seals and puffins and in recent years seen pods of dolphins, up close and personal, which is a truly amazing experience.

Herm Island is just a three-mile boat ride away and is a regular place for us to visit. This special little Island has a lovely hotel, great restaurants, and amazing beaches. The sun in Herm is special, and people often talk about getting a Herm tan as the air there seems clearer than anywhere else in the Bailiwick of Guernsey.

My son works for Sark Shipping occasionally and he regularly sees dolphins on his trips to Sark.

His links with Sark gave me the opportunity to have a trip there a couple of years ago and again it was a fantastic experience. My wife and I enjoyed a carriage ride, a great stay at Stocks Hotel and several walks around the quiet, car free, Sark 'roads'.

Memorable days which will remain with us for the rest of our lives.

With friends in Alderney, and our favourite Channel Island hotel located there, we need little excuse to visit that Island too. During 2022 a new boat service was introduced making it even easier to get to the Northern Isle.

And of course, Jersey is just a ten-minute flight away (one flight we had in December 2019 took just 7 minutes) and well worth a visit if you have some spare time during your stay in Guernsey.

In fact, all the Islands are beautiful, and the environment changes with the seasons. The weather and the direction of the wind contribute to the ambience, so no two days are ever the same. We have cliffs, beaches, walks and history in abundance. All within a few square miles.

You can work out, wear yourself out or relax in resplendent peace and quiet – the choice is yours. Guernsey and its Bailiwick can be what you want it to be. You just need to know what you want and where to look for it.

Hopefully, this Handbook will help you plan your trip to Guernsey, and ensure you enjoy your perfect holiday.

The sections covered in this book include:

About the Handbook
An Introduction to Guernsey
Travelling to Guernsey
Where to Stay
What to See and Do in Guernsey
Experience Guernsey Month by Month
Eating Out
Shopping
Guernsey Folklore
Guernsey and the World

About the Handbook

This is the ninth edition of this Handbook which evolved out of the successful Guide to Guernsey which I guess makes this our twelfth edition.

This Handbook is constantly evolving in the light of comments and advice we have received, and this year we have added some extra images and an extra section for you to enjoy.

We hope you will really love reading all about our Island and if you choose to visit, have a wonderful time while you are there.

These Handbooks are designed to provide information about the Island which the visitor can use as a reference. In a new section we will set out what happens in Guernsey during the year as experienced by the locals.

I have inserted more web links so those with access to wifi, or who have the 4G and 5G enabled Kindles, can use the browser to link to the various websites we list.

As the Kindle Fire and later models are now widespread, I shall also include more photographs of the Island so that you can get a better idea of what Guernsey is like.

All visitors to Guernsey should visit the Guernsey Information Centre, as soon as they can, to see what is happening during their stay. At the visitor Information Centre, they also have a great range of local books and souvenirs if you want to take presents home for the family.

Most Hotels and Guest Houses will also have racks of brochures giving you a good idea of what there is to do.

As soon as you arrive, whether it be at the Airport or Harbour, you should pick up the Essential Guernsey free map of the Island which will help you find your way around. They also produce an excellent guide where many of the local attractions are promoted.

If you do intend to drive, please take note of the section in this Guide on driving in Guernsey. There are many different rules which you need to be aware of as soon as you drive away from the Harbour or Airport.

Yellow stop lines and Filter in Turn junctions are the most important elements you certainly need to be aware of as they can cause accidents for those who don't know how they work.

Please remember that the maximum speed limit on the island is 35 mph. Around the towns it is 25mph and in some areas around schools it can be 20mph.

When you are at the Guernsey Information Centre, pick up a parking clock as many parking areas, especially in St Peter Port, have timed parking and you will need to set your clock when you park. Parking is free but the clock costs a few pounds.

Within the Handbook we offer you some ideas as to what to do on a day out. There are loads of things to do in Guernsey so, please, as suggested, visit the Guernsey Information Centre, and see what is on offer during your stay. Look out for the events diary which will give you some idea of the festivals and events that are going on while you are on the Island.

In the past we have tried to include as many dates of events as possible, however in recent years we have included a monthly diary as dates often change and new events are added. We recommend you look at the online events diary before you visit the Island which can be found on the www.visitguernsey.com website before you book your journey.

In the past, Visit Guernsey produced a printed event diary which could be found in all hotels, guest houses and self-catering accommodation. I'm not sure if this is being printed in 2024.

The aim of this Handbook is designed to help you enjoy and make the most of your visit to Guernsey.

An Introduction to the Location, History and Culture of Guernsey

Located in the Bay of St Malo, on the edge of the English Channel, Guernsey is less than a hundred miles south of the English south coast and thirty or so miles from the French Coast.

It is around 24 square miles in area, with one airport and a main harbour, which caters for passenger and freight traffic. It also has a smaller harbour in St Sampsons, which is used for materials such as coal and fuel.

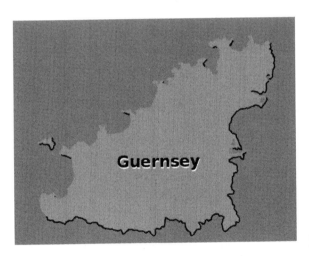

Guernsey is part of a Bailiwick, a group of Islands under the control of a Bailiff. The Bailiff is the head of the legal system. The other Islands in the group include Alderney, Sark, Herm, Breqhou and Jethou. Guernsey is a short, 10-minute flight from Jersey, the largest of the Channel Islands, and a separate jurisdiction.

The History of Guernsey is as long as it is unique and fascinating. Guernsey became an Island about 10,000 years ago when the land bridge to France succumbed to rising sea levels. Evidence of Neolithic man has been found dating back over 8,000 years and the many burial mounds, dolmens and menhirs on the Island are some of the oldest in Europe.

There are three Dolmens on the Island that you can walk into, the best being the Dehus Dolmen at Bordeaux in the North of the Island. Iron Age man settled on the Island and the Romans also used Guernsey as a useful staging post when crossing the Channel.

Ownership of property on the Island helps us understand some of its history, with records dating back to before 1066.

The lands of Normandy in France were at one time under the control of the Bretons. These lands were taken over by Vikings, under the leadership of Rollo.

Their conquests led to the creation of the Duchy of Normandy which included the Channel Islands.

It is conceivable that when William the Conqueror, the Duke of Normandy, invaded England and fought Harold at the Battle of Hastings in 1066, that people from the Islands were part of his army. Certainly, after the battle, Guernsey landowners also became owners of land in England. In time that would impact on the future nationality of the Islands and the prosperity the Islands enjoy today.

As part of the Duchy of Normandy, the Islands existed in relative peace and tranquility for many years, but in time France was reunited and, in the agreement made by King John and Phillippe Augustus of France in 1204, the Islands were forgotten.

The story is told that the wealthy landowners were asked to decide if the Islands wanted to remain as part of Great Britain or France. It seems the landowners must have had more interests in England than France as they chose to be part of Great Britain.

The Islands have remained British ever since, despite rare attempts by the French to seize them back. The arrangement was officially recognised in 1254, when the Islands were annexed to the Crown of England.

As a reward for their loyalty to the British Crown, the Islands were given the right to make their own laws. That moment in history has allowed the Islands to retain their status as Crown Dependencies, answerable to the British Monarchy rather than the British Government.

With the ongoing threat of French attacks, many fortifications were built to protect the Island. The most spectacular of these is Castle Cornet which guards the harbour of St Peter Port. Work on that Castle began around 1204 and for most of its history it remained a short boat ride away from the Island.

Castle Cornet, St Peter Port.

The Castle's most active period was probably during the English Civil War when it remained loyal to the Crown while the Island sided with Cromwell. Periodic shelling took place, but the story goes that, as the Commander of the garrison in the Castle owned property in St Peter Port, targets were selected very carefully!

The Castle remained loyal to the Crown throughout the Civil War, being supplied by sea from Jersey. As a mark of that loyalty, and I believe by Royal command, the Union Jack, as opposed to the Guernsey flag, is always flown from the flagstaff at the top of the Castle.

The next period of intense defence building came when Napoleon began his reign in France and conquered large swathes of Europe. The Islanders firmly believed they could be invaded at any time and as such the garrison on the Island was strengthened, as were the defences.

At that time, the Island was actually two Islands with the Northern part separated from the main Island by the Braye. There was a physical bridge linking the two Islands situated where St Sampsons Harbour is now. That shopping area is still known locally as 'The Bridge'.

To ensure that troops could be moved quickly to the Northern defences in the event of an attack, the Braye was filled in and the Military Road was created. That road is still, I believe, the longest and straightest road on the Island.

Other larger roads were created to move troops to the West Coast and these 'major' roads remain the Island's main thoroughfares to this day.

In the event, all this activity proved a suitable deterrent and Guernsey never came under attack. An interesting side story is that thousands of Russian troops were rested on the Island during the Napoleonic War.

They were billeted on what is now Delancey Park near my old home – it seems amazing to think that 200 years ago thousands of Russian troops were living on that park within a few yards of where I used to live, maybe even on the land where my house was built.

A few of them died while they were here and a small graveyard near the Vale Castle marks the spot where they were buried.

As a location, the Islands didn't feature in the First World War, but at the time Guernsey had its own Militia which fought bravely on the Western front. Members of The Militia or Royal Guernsey Light Infantry as it was called during the Great War, died in large numbers in the trenches at Passchendaele, Cambrai and then at the Battle of Lys.

After they returned from the First World War what was left of the militia was disbanded. Efforts were made to restart it and a small force was created between the wars, but this was disbanded in 1940 for the duration of the 2nd World War.

Many of those men went on to fight in the British armed forces but the Militia would not reform again.

Much of the history of the militia and the defence of Guernsey is portrayed in Castle Cornet and the many excellent museums around the Island.

Fort Grey, off Guernsey's West Coast

The Island's strategic position between England and France, and its strong trading and nautical history, has made the Island an important location and worth defending.

When travelling around Guernsey you can't miss the various forts and Castles which date back over 800 years.

Arguably, however, even more striking are the German defences left after the Occupation of the Islands during the Second World War.

The Channel Islands were the only British territories in the European theatre of operations to be occupied by the Germans during the Second World War. The Occupation lasted for 5 years, and the occupiers invested heavily in defending the Islands to ensure they would not be recaptured.

Large numbers of German troops were garrisoned on the Islands, and Alderney was used as a concentration camp. Over 100 German soldiers died on the Island over the 5 years and a Military Cemetery at Fort George became their final resting place.

Since the Second World War the Island has enjoyed a period of stability and growth. After the war, the tomato growing industry flourished, but this declined in the eighties and Finance took over as the dominant sector, supported by a strong manufacturing sector.

In recent years Finance has continued to grow and is now supported by a mix of tourism, creative, manufacturing, IT, and a myriad of smaller industries.

The Government of Guernsey is carried out by the States of Deliberation, which consists of 38 members from Guernsey, elected by the residents. There are no party politics, although a few alliances have been established over the last year.

Each member stands for election by their own manifesto. You can see how the States of Guernsey is made up on this website - www.gov.gg/deputies

The Island is split into ten parishes, and each has a certain amount of control over such things as refuse collection, street lighting and the like. In 2020, Guernsey saw the introduction of Island Wide Voting which enabled Islanders to select up to 38 Deputies to represent them in the States of Guernsey.

The last election took place in June 2020, and went surprisingly well. The 2024 election will be held on the same basis, although some deputies are looking to change the system.

The States of Guernsey is divided into Departments, each responsible for different aspects of the Islands management, such as Education, Health, and the Environment. Each Department is headed up by a President.

Full details of how the States is run can be found on the www.gov.gg website.

With such strong links to France, the Island has retained its own patois language, closely linked to Norman French. Usage is limited these days though attempts to revive it through the Islands school children are being made.

Guernsey Laws also have their origin in Norman Law and local Advocates (lawyers) must complete the Certificat d'EtudesJuridiques Françaises et Normandes from Caen University. The final exam is conducted in French.

Road names and house names in the Island are still mostly in French.

Over the last 50 years the Island landscape has changed in many ways. The demise of the tomato industry left many derelict greenhouses on the Island while the growth of the Finance Industry has seen the construction of many new office buildings in and around the Island's capital, St Peter Port.

However, the local planners have confined most new development to the areas around St Peter Port, St Sampson's and the North of Guernsey, leaving the south of the Island, and the southern cliffs almost unchanged over the last few decades.

The people of Guernsey are, by and large, friendly, and hospitable. Around 63,000 people live on the Island and the majority are local. They are hardworking and often have more than one job.

Fishing, horticulture, retailing, and traditional trades are still strong on the Island. If you are lost and need help, just ask. You will be surprised just how helpful some people can be.

Herm Harbour at low tide.

It isn't unknown for people to give lifts or to say follow me to show visitors the way they want to go.

To be honest the Island is also so small, once you find your way to the coast, you will find it quite easy to get around.

The Bus service is great too and the new buses include stop by stop information, so you will know where to get off. If you are unsure just ask the driver for help. There aren't many places that you can't get to easily, either by bus or on foot.

How to Get to Guernsey

As an Island, Guernsey has developed a range of air and sea links offering the visitor several options. By sea there are fast ferry services from Poole on the south coast of England, with a slower, all-weather ferry operating from Portsmouth.

The latest high-speed vessel is pictured below and serves the route to Poole. Condor services was sold in 2019 to a group which includes Brittany Ferries.

It will be interesting to see if there are any changes in the future. As usual, rumours abound as to the future of the ferry service in 2024.

Condor Liberation

There are also sea links to the French Coast, again by fast ferry to St Malo and a less frequent service to the Normandy coast at Dielette. Travel to the Islands of Jersey and Alderney is also possible by sea and air. A new ferry service to Jersey is being planned for 2024. I will include more details once the outcome of those plans is known.

In 2022 a new ferry service to Alderney, operated by Alderney Ferry Services, was introduced. We used the ferry to visit Alderney in 2023 and I am hoping the service will continue to run throughout 2024.

By air you can travel from several UK Airports, directly to Guernsey. These include, at the time of writing, Gatwick, Southampton, Manchester, Birmingham, Leeds Bradford, East Midlands, Bristol, and Exeter.

Direct links also operate into Jersey and Alderney. There have been plans to introduce a regular route to Rennes in France and I am hoping this will commence during 2024.

With a single flight change you can access the Island from almost anywhere.

With the open skies policy, new routes are under consideration all the time. It is worth looking at the various websites run by the airlines to see what the current links are.

Possibly your first view of St Peter Port

Operators include:

By Sea:
Condor Ferries
www.condorferries.co.uk
0345 609 1026 (UK)

Condor Ferry leaving St Peter Port.

By Air:-
Aurigny
www.aurigny.com
01481 267267

Part of the Aurigny Fleet at Guernsey Airport

Blue Islands
www.blueislands.com
Tel: 01234 589 200

Blue Islands Aircraft at Guernsey Airport

Travel to the Island can be expensive, particularly if you wait until the last minute to book. Cheap seats are normally available for bookings made well in advance, making the Islands far more affordable than commonly thought.

However, with all the competition brought about by the open skies policy, prices can be competitive on some routes, so look out for the good deals.

When booking air travel online be sure to check out the full price, including airport taxes, baggage, and allocated seating as this can increase the cost of the flights considerably.

When travelling by sea, the ferries from the UK can accommodate vehicles. Bringing your car to Guernsey can be an attractive option, but if your stay is short, it may be cheaper to hire a car when on the Island.

Hire car companies include:
Value Car Hire – 01481 243547
Europcar (Harlequin Hire Cars) - 01481 239696
Hertz – 01481 239516

We will discuss getting around Guernsey later in the Guide as there are some very different driving rules on the Island roads which you need to know about before getting into your car.

You can also bring motorbikes and cycles to Guernsey on the ferry but again both can be hired on the Island.

Guernsey Airport at night

Where to Stay?

There is a wide range of Hotels, Guest Houses and Self-Catering options for you to consider if you plan to stay in Guernsey. Prices are available to suit every pocket, and a comprehensive list of accommodation is available on the Visit Guernsey web site at www.visitguernsey.com

However, we have several that we think are worth consideration, not because we have any interest in them but because we like the location and the facilities they have to offer.

On the West Coast of the Island is the Cobo Bay Hotel. If you choose this hotel, try and get a room with a balcony overlooking Cobo Bay. It may cost extra but if you are lucky enough to enjoy one or two of the spectacular Guernsey sunsets while you are on the Island, it will be worth every penny.

One of the more exclusive hotels was La Grande Mare Hotel, also on the Island's West Coast, this time at Vazon Bay. It is currently undergoing a complete rebuild and as I understand it, may not be offering accommodation in the future. Certainly, it will not be operational in 2024.

I believe the 18-hole Golf Course, golf shop, indoor swimming pool with gym and health club are still operational.

Probably the best hotel for the south coast bays and cliffs in our view is the Bella Luce.

If you want to spend your time in the Island's capital, St Peter Port, the Old Government House Hotel (OGH) and Moore's Hotel would be good choices. The OGH is the better of the two in terms of facilities with an excellent Health Club and restaurant. Over the last few years they have set up an annual Christmas Alpine Lodge each December and hopefully they will do so again in 2024.

We've also heard good reports about the friendliness of the owners and staff of the Duke of Normandie Hotel which is in the heart of town. It's linked to the Pickled Pig Gastro pub which is a real bonus.

All the Hotels we mention have excellent restaurants and are renowned for their good service.

Slightly further out of town is the Duke of Richmond Hotel, where we have enjoyed many a lovely meal. It is close to the Island's main Leisure Centre and Cambridge Park.

Close by is La Fregate Hotel, which is renowned for its first-class service. We enjoyed a short staycation there in 2023 and the room and service were spectacular. On the southern outskirts of town is the Hotel de Havelet, which has wonderful views over St Peter Port Harbour and Castle Cornet.

Out of town you have a choice of beautiful country hotels, each with their own attributes. One of our favourites is the St Pierre Park Hotel, which has a nine-hole par 3 golf course with a modern driving range and a new pirate themed crazy golf course.

We stayed there several times over the last few years. It is very handy in terms of buses going into and out of town, and for buses to the west coast beaches. We walked into town a few times; but be aware the hill is a bit steep. The traffic is quite heavy too, so if you are not comfortable walking, take the bus.

Breakfast was excellent, and the room was very comfortable.

Sitting on the Balcony with a glass of wine watching the sunset over the large pond and gardens is nothing short of spectacular.

St Pierre Park Pond at Sunset

Other hotels include La Trelade, La Villette, the Hougue Du Pommier, La Barbarie, the Jerbourg Hotel (on the cliffs), Les Douvres and the Farmhouse.

One of the newer hotels on the Island, designed originally for the over 50's, but not exclusively so, is the Fermain Valley Hotel. The food there is exceptional, and they have one of the finest restaurants on Guernsey attached to the Hotel. In the top part of the hotel is the exceptional Buho Mexican restaurant.

They also have Escape Rooms if you are feeling adventurous.

We stayed at the Fermain Valley just before Christmas at the end of 2014, and a few times since, and I can say with confidence that the rooms are beautifully designed, and the facilities were brilliant. They have an impressive heated indoor pool so don't forget your bathers.

Despite it being December, we enjoyed a cliff walk, then a swim in their pool and later a wonderful meal in their nautical themed restaurant.

Sunrise over Jersey

The next morning, we sat on our balcony and watched the sun rise over Jersey.

Breakfast was amazing and the staff couldn't have been more helpful. A very special hotel.

We also had the opportunity to stay at the Peninsula Hotel in 2019 as our daughter got married there. The restaurant had just been refurbished and I believe they are starting to refurbish the rooms. It is in a lovely location in the North of the Island with spectacular views from some of the rooms across Grand Havre Bay.

The beach is literally a few minutes' walk away from the front, and the back, of the hotel, so if you like to feel the sand between your toes this is the hotel for you. The staff were wonderful.

We stayed at the Farmhouse Hotel a few years ago. Located near the Airport, the rooms were very well appointed, and the meals were wonderful. You don't have sea views from this hotel and the pool wasn't open when we were there, but I would say the food was as excellent, if not better than the Fermain Valley, especially the choice for breakfast.

An exciting new development for Guernsey was the construction of a Premier Inn hotel in a prime East Coast location. This was completed during 2022 and bookings are available online.

The Premier Inn

If you are wondering how locals can use some of these hotels and stay over, particularly in the winter months, it is because there are often deals where you can sample these wonderful hotels and restaurants at bargain prices.

It is worth checking the hotel websites when you are planning your visit as you might get the chance to take advantage of one of these offers and enjoy a nice meal out for less than the normal price.

A list of the hotels I've mentioned and other hotels, together with their phone numbers is set out in the appendices.

Guest Houses on Guernsey are reducing in number, but a few good ones are still available, and a list of our favourites is in the appendices.

Self-Catering Bungalows are a popular choice in Guernsey, and though they too have reduced in number, there are several still available.

Vazon Bay Holiday Apartments

The Vazon Bay Apartments are a popular choice and the 4-star Wisteria Apartments attached to the Fleur du Jardin Hotel look excellent. They are both nicely located, being just a short walk from the West Coast beaches.

The Vazon Bay Apartments are more suited to families and are within yards of the Island's West Coast. They have their own pool and are next to a very popular restaurant called Crabby Jacks.

The same applies to those at the Collinette Hotel which is an easy walk from the Islands main shopping area of St Peter Port.

We recently visited the Albany apartments as our son stayed there for a while in a winter let. They are excellent and within easy walking distance of the town centre.

A full list of self-catering apartments is available on the Visit Guernsey web site but listed in the appendices are the contact details for some of those that we would suggest, simply by location and reputation.

L'Aumone House Barn

Camping

The main campsites in Guernsey are listed below for those who like holidays under canvas. One site is also a haven for those who prefer a little extra comfort when they camp.

If you want to bring your mobile home to Guernsey, you need to check with the campsite first as I believe only a limited number of pitches are available.

Please check availability before making any firm travel arrangements.

The sites are:

Camp de Reves Glamping	01481 415640
Fauxquets Valley Farm	01481 255460
Vaugrat Campsite	07781 413274
La Bailloterie, Vale	01481 243636

Keeping in Touch

Most hotels will offer you free wifi during your stay, but if you like to catch up with the news and access the internet while drinking a cup of tea or coffee there are a couple of places we would recommend.

Along 'the front' between the roundabout with the ships mast and Salerie Corner, heading north, you will find Muse, which offers free wifi, meals and excellent teas and coffees.

If you like Italian surroundings, Otto, just north of town, near the Longstore offers free wifi and excellent tea and coffee, plus a full menu.

Another excellent option is Cocos, which is situated at the southern end of the bus terminus. They close on Mondays. In Market Square there is a lovely small café called the Café Delice which is popular with the tech people or for business meetings.

Now you have no excuse for not checking Facebook and telling the world what a fabulous holiday you are having!

If you are visiting, and plan to do some work while you are here, and need a base for a few hours a day or week then look no further than the Digital Greenhouse. This is a space designed to encourage the development of Digital Businesses on the Island and places are available to rent for short periods.

If you need somewhere to plug in your computer, enjoy great wifi, and continue with your blog or whatever you are working on, in a fun business environment, check out the Digital Greenhouse.

To find out more about this excellent facility, visit www.digitalgreenhouse.gg

The Guernsey Markets include the offices of the Guernsey Chamber of Commerce. If you are a Chamber member, they might be able to offer you somewhere to work from. The Market has an inner street which again is somewhere dry to work on a rainy day.

What to See and Do in Guernsey?

There are many things to see and do in Guernsey for people of all ages and whatever your interests. If you would like to explore the scenic aspect of the Island, you can walk the cliffs, wander through the lanes, or visit the beaches.

Some places are a must see, like Castle Cornet, Fort Grey, Victor Hugo's House, the Little Chapel, and the Occupation Museums. Hidden prehistoric Dolmens, secluded bays and sites of special ecological significance can be harder to find but well worth the effort.

For the kids there is Oaty and Joeys Playbarn at Oatlands which is open all year round.

At certain times of the year there are areas worthy of a visit. At the end of April and early May the Bluebell Woods on the Island's East coast can be spectacular. The cliffs in spring are also amazing with a riot of colourful flowers and gorse in full bloom.

The Bluebell Woods

If you want to see Puffins, they nest in Herm during the spring. The best way to see them is with Island Rib Voyages and if you are on the sea, you may be lucky enough to see dolphins around our East Coast. Their numbers are increasing year on year.

Tours of the Island can be arranged by taxi or through the tour operators. One unique experience is through Tour Guernsey in their safari style landrover. They will take you to see many of the interesting places and some of the tours are specific such as Occupation tours. I believe there is a Guernsey Literary and Potato Peel Pie Society tour now.

They will also take you to the usual Tourist attractions such as Guernsey Pearl, Oatlands, and Guernsey Candles.

While these can be worth a visit if you are hunting for souvenirs, they are also easily found and are not the hidden treasures that taxi firms can show you and which many visitors never see.

If you are interested in prehistoric history, it is worth seeking out the Dehus Dolmen at Bordeaux. There you can enter the grave chamber and by using the lighting put in place just for the purpose, highlight the carving in one of the large stones which form the roof.

Just watch your head as you enter the chamber, it is very low.

Entrance to Le Creux es Faies, Dolmen at L'Eree

When you visit Guernsey, there are often special events you should look out for. The Guernsey Event Diary will give you details of such events and can be found on the www.visitguernsey.com website.

You can also get an up-to-date view on what is happening during your stay by visiting the Guernsey Information Centre on the seafront in the heart of St Peter Port.

Look out for special exhibitions at the Guernsey Museum in Candie Gardens.

On May the 9th the Island celebrates the anniversary of Liberation from the German Occupation at the end of the Second World War. Special events are held each year to mark the occasion, which if you are in the Island at that time, you can enjoy. 2024 will be the 79th anniversary of Liberation.

Something which was introduced in 2020 were Tuk Tuk Tours. They do Christmas Lights tours in December and in the season from Easter until the end of October, they offer various options for tours from Town Tours to full Coastal tours.

Full details can be found on their website www.tuktukguernsey.co.uk

Guernsey Tuk Tuks, image courtesy of Tuk Tuk Guernsey

To highlight what goes on we will take you through the Guernsey Experience on a month-by-month basis, explaining what is happening and giving you our experiences of the various events, we have enjoyed over the past few years.

Also, your hotel will have a Tourist Information Board, full of ideas if you are short of anything to do.

Experience Guernsey

Month by Month

January

January is usually a quiet month, in common with many other places in the Northern hemisphere. After the celebrations of Christmas and the New Year, people tend to hunker down until the next pay day and let the bad weather pass them by. Once one or two pay packets have restored their bank accounts, then they will start going out and enjoying themselves again.

That is unless the January sales in St Peter Port tempt you to part with your hard-earned cash in search of a bargain.

Ice-skating is available over the Christmas period until early January at the spectacular Friquet Garden Centre. Don't break a leg!

The popular Alpine Lodge will still be running at the OGH Hotel for the first week of January to give you the opportunity to experience food and drink in an après ski setting.

January has been known to produce some spectacular weather with beautiful skies, flat seas and sharp clear air which can give you excellent views of Jersey, Alderney and further afield the coast of France.

While some restaurants close for a few weeks, people are out walking on the beaches and the cliffs, strolling around the lanes and the parks, and generally burning off a few of those extra calories that were put on during the festivities.

Cold water swimming has become quite popular on the Island and you will see people swimming at the bathing pools or in most of the island's most popular bays, all year round.

The big spring tides enable Islanders to go ormering, which will make headlines in the local paper dependent on the size of the catches. 2024 has seen some excellent catches by some of the more hardy locals.

Ormers are a type of abalone and Guernsey is the furthest north you will find this delicacy. For some fun children's stories about Olli the Ormer, search for him on Amazon.

Many great offers are available at the hotels and restaurants that remain open, so if you do choose to visit in January, and February for that matter, you can still have a wonderful time.

You won't be sunning yourselves and getting a tan, as the temperatures drop substantially when the skies are clear, but if you are a fan of those lovely, peaceful days, when the air is crisp, and you can see for miles then Guernsey can be the place for you.

My Facebook memories from January are full of long walks, often followed by lovely meals out in front of warm fires, in short, just enjoying the good days that January and February can bring.

Obviously, it isn't always like that and there are times when it rains and blows a gale. But watching the sea throw itself against the sea walls on the west coast has a beauty of its own.

There are numerous theatrical events and shows during the winter months including a pantomime or two. The museums are open with many displays and the farmers markets are in full swing on Saturdays near the end of the month and then throughout the year.

If visiting libraries is your thing, then check out the Guilles Alles Library website at www.library.gg/events to see what's happening during your visit. There is always something happening and of course, they are a source of great information about the Island.

St James, the local concert hall, is already promoting a range of events that are being staged during 2024 and the Beau Sejour sports hall and theatre is hosting a Beyond the Barricade, the UK's longest running Musical Theatre Concert Tour on the 27th, though I understand it is already a sell out.

Also, during January there are many sporting fixtures to enjoy. Usually, Guernsey FC play their home games at Footes Lane and the Guernsey Rugby Club, also play at the same venue in their home games within the UK national leagues.

The Mallard Cinema is also a good place to enjoy the latest blockbuster on a cold and windy winters evening.

The Guernsey Arts Commission diary is also a source of many local events covering everything from Pottery painting to crafts and coffee mornings. The popular open mic nights are also listed on their website at www.arts.gg

The Princess Royal Centre for the Performing Arts also has a range of events on during the month, including We Will Rock You performed by the Elizabeth College Theatre Company. You can find this, and a host of other events, on www.guernseytickets.gg.

February

The Island will still be gripped by the chills of winter during February but again there will be good days and already it will feel noticeably warmer as the month goes on.

Those Islanders who still run greenhouses will be planting away and the sports events will be in full swing throughout the month as the winter season nears its end.

The Visit Guernsey diary for February 2024 is a bit scant at the time of writing. Check out the St James, Performing Arts and Beau Sejour links as detailed in January to see what is happening in those locations.

Hopefully, the walking tours will return soon. Having taken a local walking tour myself I can highly recommend these events, which are thoroughly interesting and good exercise. A hearty meal in a town restaurant or a warming drink in the Ship and Crown are highly recommended after all that exercise.

In 2016, we visited the beautiful Fermain Valley Hotel for Valentine's Day, and my Facebook page is full of pictures from the restaurant and of views from our room overlooking Fermain Bay to the East.

By the end of the month thoughts move to spring, daffodils are in full bloom and the gardens are starting to come to life. The sun starts to feel warm on the skin and the sun beds are put out in the garden.

If the weather isn't great, you can also see the latest cinema releases at the Mallard Cinema, near the airport or visit Oaty and Joeys with the kids, which is open all year round. A walk around the Oatlands Centre is always recommended, whatever the weather. If the sun is shining you can always try your hand on their crazy golf putting course.

The Guernsey Arts Commission is also a source of many local events and on the 5th of February 2024 they have an open mic music event at the Thomas De La Rue in their diary. You can find their events diary on their website at www.arts.gg. There is something to do in that diary, virtually every day.

One highlight, if the weather is OK, is the Guernsey Folklore Trail which will take you to 20 locations around the Island.

March

The events start to build as the days really start to warm up.

The Farmers Markets at Saumarez Manor will start in April but there are often other Markets held around the Island. There is a Facebook page for Guernsey Farmers Markets which is worth checking.

Don't forget to check the Guernsey Museums website as well as the Arts website to check for events.

With Easter at the end of the month, hopefully Island Rib Voyages will be in full swing. We have enjoyed great trips out with them over the years. When the sea is calm, and the sky is sunny and clear there is not a better experience to be had anywhere on the Island.

Inside the Sark Caves, looking out.

We have been inside the Sark Caves, which is an awesome experience and have been lucky enough to see dolphins, puffins (in season) and seals, as well as a myriad of different seabirds.

Usually at the end of the month the noon day gun will start firing again for the summer from Castle Cornet.

Always worth a visit, Castle Cornet is normally open during the summer between 10am to 5pm. There are many events held there throughout the year including outdoor concerts and re-enactments. Check the Museums.gov.gg website to ensure it is open when you are on the Island.

Castle Cornet has been part of the St Peter Port view for 800 years and was designed to protect the approach to St Peter Port Harbour.

Castle Cornet from across Havelet Bay

In Alderney you can visit the Alderney Roman Fort, called the Nunnery Heritage Site, visit Fort Doyle, or simply enjoy a well-being walk. You can see their event diary on www.visitalderney.com

Don't forget it's Mother's Day during March so book early if you want to take that special person in your life out for a celebratory meal on the 10th of the month.

April

As soon as we reach April the season really kicks off and visitor numbers will start to swell. There can be amazingly good weather at this time of year, although the evenings can still be cold. You will see people sitting outside enjoying Al Fresco dining around St Peter Port and outside some of the coastal hotels and restaurants.

With the clocks changing at the end of March the days draw out, allowing locals extra recreational time after work, as well as at the weekends. You'll notice the beaches and cliffs will start to get busy.

There are loads of Guided tours to choose from and boating becomes real fun with regular trips on Island Ribs available. Day trips to Herm and Sark have become more regular. The Guernsey Marathon usually attracts runners from off Island. It is being held on the 14th of April. Check out www.guernsey-marathon.com.

Easter is early this year and is usually the time that many attractions re-open their doors as visitor numbers swell. That means most, if not all the locations around the island will be open all month.

The marinas usually start to get busy and with luck the first cruise ships start to appear. The Petit Train starts its tours around St Peter Port at Easter and the ringing of its bell marks the sound of spring in St Peter Port.

Victor, the Petit Train

In April, the Visit Guernsey diary will start to fill. During the month, for those interested in history there will be walking tours associated with the upcoming celebration of Liberation Day.

The 23rd April will see the start of the Guernsey Literary Festival. It will run until the 5th of May. Full details of all the events can be found on www.guernseyliteraryfestival.com.

Tuk Tuk tours should also be starting so have a look at their website to see what will be available in 2024. www.tuktukguernsey.co.uk.

It's also a good time to think about a visit to Herm. As the days get warmer the beauty of spring in Herm is not to be underestimated.

A Trident ferry leaving for Herm from St Peter Port

May

The month of May marks the 79th Anniversary of Liberation Day and this is celebrated on Thursday the 9th of May.

The popular Seafront Sundays begin around this time. These are themed events held on the Crown pier and along the sea front from the main roundabout as far as the Town Church. Each event includes local crafts and food products as well as the theme for the event.

The themes can be local food, motor sport, pets, sport and the like. They are held throughout the summer, the last usually taking place around the end of August or early September.

Seafront Sunday Open Air Craft Market

If you get a chance, make sure you visit the Bluebell woods above Fermain Bay at the start of May or the end of April to see this annual natural spectacular, provided by mother nature.

Liberation Day in Guernsey marks the day the German Occupying forces surrendered to the British Military ending 5 long years of occupation. Most years there is a cavalcade to mark the event as well as numerous other functions. The whole day usually culminates with a firework display in St Peter Port.

In Alderney, they don't celebrate Liberation Day as we do in Guernsey.

Because of the damage to the Island and the fact that there was a concentration camp on the Island, the Alderney residents weren't allowed to return to their homes until December 1945. So, they hold a celebration in December each year to mark Homecoming Day.

Many major sporting events are held in May each year, including the Muratti, which is the climax of the Channel Island football calendar.

The match is usually between Guernsey and Jersey, but there is a semi-final when Alderney take on one of the two main Islands. They haven't played in a final since 1938 when the system was different. Alderney haven't won the trophy since 1920.

GU36 – The Guernsey Ultra is being held on the 19th of May. For all fitness fans this is the ultimate test of fitness and stamina as it combines mixed terrain in a 36-mile race around the Island.

The annual Guernsey Literary Festival will be in full swing from the start of the month. It runs from the 23rd of April until the 5th of May. This celebration of writing is a great event for all the budding authors out there or for people who are just interested in hearing writers talk about their work and their lives.

You can find out what is happening on their website at www.guernseyliteraryfestival.com/

With several Bank Holidays in May the Islanders usually take full advantage with events like the Balcony Gigs at the Cobo Bay Hotel, Hill Climb motor racing on the Val des Terres and of course all the events surrounding Liberation Day.

The spring walking festival of events usually start in May.

A legacy of the pandemic is the Guernsey Together Festival which will be held over multiple dates during the summer.

If you happen to be in Herm on the 25th of May, you can watch Britain's Premier Ska Band - Skabucks.

At the end of the month on the 25th and 26th there is a Guernsey Together Music Festival. Tickets usually go on sale around the end of January, and you can see the full line up and venue details on their website at www.guernseytogether.co.uk .

June

Now the weather really hots up and events crop up thick and fast. Island Rib Voyages can take you to see our Atlantic Grey Seal colony – see below - and it will be your last chance to see the puffins in Puffin Bay at the back of Herm Island before they head out into the Atlantic.

Sea Front Sundays carry on through the month, and if the sun shines the atmosphere can be brilliant with loads of stalls and Al Fresco dining filling the sea front for this popular event.

A Cider and Ale Festival is usually held in Herm during June but so far dates are yet to be announced. They do have a Supersonic Queen concert scheduled for the 22nd of June featuring one of the UK's premier Queen tribute bands. At the end of the month, you can take part in their one of their popular Haunted Herm Ghost tours.

Bloomin' Alderney starts on the 3rd of June and runs through to the 9th of June. The Guernsey Floral Festival is usually held in June too.

The annual Battle of Britain air display also takes place in June this year on Thursday the 13th. Hopefully with the Red Arrows this year.

There is usually a classic vehicle show in Saumarez Park during the month which is always a good event. This is one of many excellent events in this lovely park setting.

The Saffery Rotary Walk will be held on the 8th of June this year. It follows a 39-mile course around the Island and is one of the Islands biggest charity fundraising events.

Dolphins off the East Coast of Guernsey

July

In July there will be Sark Fest 2024, which starts on the 5th of July for three days. As well as the music in Sark, Castle Cornet is alive with music as the ever-popular KPMG Castle Nights will usually be held in either July or August.

In past years these have been held over several consecutive Fridays, these free to attend events are loved by locals and visitors alike, with many people taking picnics and spending the evenings sitting on blankets in the Castle grounds listening to a diverse range of music in these historic surroundings. Doors open at 6pm and the events go on until about 9pm.

Guernsey's traditional show, the Viaer Marchi starts the show season off on the first Monday in July – in 2024 this will be the 1st of July. There you will see traditional crafts, Guernsey Dancing, historical displays as well as loads of food and drink stands and other stalls with a local flavor.

It is well known that the sun always shines on the Viaer Marchi (well almost always) and this traditional event attracts people in their thousands. It is held in Saumarez Park, starting at 5pm.

Guernsey people are also big supporters of local charities and an event called 30 Bays in 30 Days has become a regular part of the calendar where people set out to swim in thirty different bays during the month in support of Les Bourgs Hospice. Fun runs and all sorts of events are held in the summer.

As a visitor I am not suggesting you participate in such events but if you are wondering what is happening on certain days when you see people running or walking along the coast in wild get-ups it won't come as such a shock! It's all for charity.

Seafront Sundays are regular events in July and August so look out for those and the balcony gigs at Cobo and other concerts are a frequent occurrence.

The National Hillclimb comes to the Val des Terres, just south of the Bus Terminus, on the 20th of July and quite often it is followed by the Motorsport Seafront Sunday. So, if you are a petrol head and like watching fast cars and bikes, make a note in the diary to visit that weekend.

The Guernsey Motorcycle and Car Club also run a series of events for those interested in travelling a little faster than the Island's speed limit. Beach racing, sprints and motorcycle trials feature on their calendar which can be found on www.gmccc.gg/events.

Every year new events are put on and if you are in the Island make sure you try to enjoy them. In recent years we enjoyed a picnic in Candie Gardens listening to a Beatles tribute band called the Day Trippers as well as watching a Soapbox race on St Julian's Avenue which was great fun.

The Harbour Carnival organised by the Round Table usually takes place in July and is always a fun event. It included a massive duck race, dinghy races, tug of war and my favourite, the Man Powered Flight contest. You can see the pictures on the Facebook page. Their website is http://www.harbourcarnival.gg/ so keep watch to see when it is going to happen in 2024.

At the end of the month the annual Scarecrow Festival is held in Torteval starting in the fields adjacent to Torteval Church. As you pass through the sign posted route you will see many scarecrow tableaus on display portraying historical figures both international and local to the Island, often in humorous settings.

Scarecrow Tableau

As part of the walk, you will be given the chance to vote for your favourites. There is also a beer tent and food available as well as a number of small stalls offering souvenirs, plants, bric-a-brac and tombolas.

In 2024 the Rocquaine regatta will be held on the 27th of July. This involves a lot of fun on the beach and in the water and of course there is always the beer tent and if you like a gamble, there is the ever-popular Crown and Anchor.

You can follow what happens at the Regatta on Facebook at
https://www.facebook.com/Rocquaine.Regatta/

In Sark the annual sheep racing event is being held on the 19th and 20th of July. On the 29th of July the Guernsey Street Festival takes place which fills St Peter Port with music until the 3rd of August.

August

The Guernsey Street Festival continues until the 3rd of the month and the Guernsey Seafront Sundays will continue as do the Guided walks, and of course the Island Rib Voyages trips, Petit Train and Tuk Tuks.

From the 5th to the 10th of August, Alderney celebrates Alderney Week with a packed diary which includes a whole range of events including music, parades, raft races and much more. We visited Alderney during Alderney week, and it is certainly a busy and fun time in the Northern Isle. Book early though, as hotel space is in short supply during that time.

Just before that, Alderney plays host to Rock the Rock, a fun-filled Charity event organized by the Alderney Rock Trust. It takes place on the 3rd of August.

August is best known in Guernsey for the shows, starting with the South Show centred around the St Martins Community centre, then the West Show on the 14th and 15th of August out at L'Eree and then finally the North Show at Saumarez Park on the 21st and 22nd. That show includes the Guernsey Battle of Flowers and all the fun of the fair.

The annual Donkey Derby also takes place in Saumarez Park on the 17th of August, which is another fun event.

If you are on the Island during this month, you should try and visit one of these shows to get a flavour of Guernsey life. For me, 'West is Best' as the phrase goes and that is the show I like to visit. The North probably claims the biggest attendance, thanks mainly to the Battle of Flowers.

At the end of the month (25th) the Vale Earth Fair will take place. It is an open-air music festival at the Vale Castle. For the music fans amongst you there is usually a Balcony Gig at the Cobo Bay hotel as part of the Bank Holiday weekend.

Pirate Bay Adventure Golf at St Pierre Park

September

There is usually another Ale and Cider event in Herm in early September, these are very popular events so if you intend to stay in Herm during this period, book early.

Channel Island Pride takes place in Guernsey on the 7th September this year. This pan Island event is always a colourful and popular event.

In fact, despite the schools going back there are loads of events taking place during the month. The walks should continue with the Autumn Walking Festival starting in September and running, or walking, until October. This includes a huge variety of walks in several locations, which I hope will include walks in and around Herm.

October

The Autumn walking festival usually continues into October, just, but inevitably as the weather takes a turn for the worse and the evenings draw in the number of events start to decline and many of those that continue go indoors.

The Tennerfest starts in October and goes on to mid-November. This is where dozens of local restaurants and hotels across the Islands offer a range of fixed menus for anything from £10 to £25.

This is a popular event and brings people out to the eateries in their thousands during what could be a quiet time for all the venues.

For the locals you can go Pumpkin Picking at Le Hechet Farm. If you've brought your car to the Island, maybe you'll want to take a Guernsey Pumpkin back home as a memory of your visit.

Many of the Museum exhibitions continue so please keep an eye on the Visit Guernsey website for the most up to date details where you can search for events at different times of the year. You can also see what is on during the week of your visit.

The website is www.visitguernsey.com

November and December

As Tennerfest comes to an end, the Christmas season starts to kick in with businesses organising their Christmas events and the shops setting out their Christmas produce.

Santa Claus turns on the lights at the beginning of December which includes the Tree of Joy at the main roundabout at the bottom of St Julians Avenue.

St Peter Port and St Sampsons are both decorated with Christmas Trees and lights for the festive occasion and early in December Father Christmas usually visits and turns on the lights.

Smith Street Christmas Lights

There are many Christmas Fairs organized by local charities where arts and crafts as well as artisan bakers get the chance to sell their wares.

Late-night shopping sessions take place on Thursday nights in St Peter Port and Tuesday nights on the Bridge.

In 2023 the Friquet Garden Centre set up an excellent Ice Rink which proved very popular, and in the past, we have enjoyed a visit to the Alpine Lodge, set up by the OGH Hotel, complete with selfie ski lift and snow drifting down outside the 'window'.

The last time we visited the Alpine Lodge the mulled cider was excellent, and the schnapps went down a treat as well as the food which included an excellent apple strudel.

We also enjoyed a meal and drinks in some outside Domes which were set up by the Duke of Richmond Hotel. The food was Scandinavian themed, and it proved a lovely evening. Hopefully it will happen again.

The Petit Train ran in 2023 taking people on tours around town to see the Christmas lights. TukTuk Guernsey also ran Christmas lights tours and will be doing the same again in 2024.

Their website is www.tuktukguernsey.co.uk.

Herm trident have also run shopping trips to Herm at the weekends for a minimal sum.

Christmas Tuk Tuks, photo by Tim Bean

In 2023 we visited Jersey for their Fete de Noue which was lovely.

If you come over for Christmas and are feeling brave, you could join the hundreds of people who enjoy a boxing day dip at Cobo Bay – not for me!! 2023 saw thousands of people taking part.

The year usually ends with a firework display at Castle Cornet and festive parties are held in St Peter Port to see the year out.

General

I haven't listed all the various walking, cycling, coasteering and kayaking tours that run throughout the summer. Again, the tourism website or a visit to the Guernsey Information Centre, when you are on the Island, will give you all the details.

Apart from events, there are many Museums and Art Galleries to visit for those interested in the history and culture of the Island.

The Guernsey Museum at Candie Gardens is the largest of the Museums. Castle Cornet has its own displays, and a guided walk of the Castle is as entertaining as it is informative.

Fort Grey on the Island's West Coast is also worth a visit as it contains displays concerning the many shipwrecks that have occurred around the Island's coast.

In fact, if you have an interest in Museums, you can buy a special ticket which will give you access to all the Government run museums during your stay.

The Guernsey Information Centre

If you like stately homes, the nearest equivalent we have in Guernsey is Sausmarez Manor. The house is well worth a visit and tours are available, including ghost tours of the House.

In the grounds is a wonderful sculpture park, as well as a model railway and tea garden. If you stop for tea do not miss out on Guernsey Gache, a local fruit loaf, which should be thickly covered with Guernsey butter.

There are regular Farmers Markets in the grounds on a Saturday s during the Spring, Summer and Autumn which are very popular.

During the Occupation of Guernsey in the Second World War, the Germans left many buildings and fortifications, some of which can be accessed during certain times of the week/year.

Memories of those years are still fresh in the minds of many of the older local generation and occasionally you might find someone who will tell you what it was like to live under German rule.

Several museums containing equipment and memorabilia from the occupation have been established, a few in bunkers and facilities left by the Germans. More bunkers are being opened all the time. You can find out more on the Festung Guernsey website at:

www.festungguernsey.supanet.com/

If you are interested in the environment, you could visit the Ramsar site, a site of special scientific importance at L'Eree and see the wonderful natural flora and fauna that is prolific in this area.

There are many other sites looked after by La Societe Guernesiaise (Tel 01481 725093) including Bird Hides and Orchid fields. You can visit their web site at www.societe.org.gg

For the more adventurous, you could try a Rib Boat Voyage. The trips include a look at the other Islands and local wildlife such as puffins and perhaps seals and dolphins if you are lucky. They also do a run along the south coast as far as the impressive Hanois Lighthouse off the tip of Pleinmont.

The views of the German defences along the south coast are impressive from the sea.

South Coast Watchtower

You can also take a tour of the Sark Coast and Caves as we did last summer and enjoy a sing song in these amazing acoustic chambers. Our daughter got engaged in the caves – see below.

Inside the Sark Caves with Island Rib Voyages

To book your place on one of these unforgettable trips visit:

http://www.islandribvoyages.com/

For the sporty, you have a choice of activities, such as Go Karting, Bowls, Golf, Fishing, Tennis, Table Tennis, Badminton, Coaststeering, Paddle Boarding, Surfing and Kayaking.

Many other sports are available at the Beau Sejour Leisure Centre. The facilities there include swimming (25 metre, 6 lane pool), table tennis, badminton, tennis, squash and much, much more. They also have a large Cinema, called Beau Cinema. To see the latest films on show visit https://www.facebook.com/beaucinema/

For the golfers there are three golf courses. Two of them are 18-hole courses, one is linked to the former Grande Mare Hotel and the other is at L'Ancresse Common. If you have a handicap, you can pay a green fee and play at both courses provided there are no competitions being run on that day.

The nine-hole course is linked to the St Pierre Park Hotel and consists of 9 tricky par threes. There is an excellent driving range attached to the course and a state-of-the-art teaching facility if you want to practice while on holiday.

If you like crazy golf, there is an excellent Pirate themed course attached to the St Pierre Park facility. It is all attached to a lovely restaurant in the grounds of the course and range called Number 19.

There is another recently refurbished crazy golf course at Oatland Village alongside the Oaty and Joey play barn which features the Joey Trislander Aircraft hanging from the ceiling. Don't forget to check out Craftwise (www.craftwise.gg) while you are there as well as the other excellent retail outlets on site.

To see all the attractions in Oatlands Village, visit their website at - https://www.oatlands.gg/

There are many excellent fishing marks around the Island coast if you would like to try a bit of sea fishing while you are in Guernsey. You can also go on organised fishing trips from the harbour of St Peter Port during the summer. Check out http://www.boatfishing.net/

There is also a surf school based at Vazon and organisations that provide outdoor adventure activities like kayaking, paddle boarding and coasteering such as Outdoor Guernsey, see their website at www.outdoorguernsey.co.uk.

Paddle Boarding in Havelet Bay

In recent years I have seen people learning to paddle board in Pembroke Bay in the north of the Island as well as kite surfing. The seas can be cold, so unless you are a hardened swimmer it might be worth bringing a wetsuit if you plan on learning to surf or paddle board, though hiring kit might be an option.

Many teams come to the Island for sports and at various times of the year sporting festivals are held. Excellent facilities exist for sports like Cricket, Football, Hockey, Rugby, Tennis and Table tennis. Guernsey hosted the Island Games in 2023.

For fishermen there is an International Bass Fishing festival which is held usually every year in August.

A trip to the small Island of Herm is also a must during the summer – take the sun cream though as the sun in Herm seems stronger than in Guernsey, probably due to the clear air, and that's no joke.

In the evenings you can enjoy the Captain's Table at the White House which includes the trip across to Herm, about three miles from St Peter Port Harbour. In the evening you can enjoy a wonderful meal in the hotel with a view back towards Guernsey, framed by the setting sun.

St Peter Port plays host to many clubs and bars for those who like a night out and you can also enjoy the latest movies at our small multi-screen cinema at the Mallard Hotel, which is located near the airport or the Beau Cinema on the outskirts of town.

Places like the Doghouse and some of the livelier bars regularly host live music and occasionally you can find outdoor entertainment, such as summer live music events and balcony concerts at the Cobo Bay Hotel.

Outside theatre is held each year at Castle Cornet, with a season of plays in this brilliant venue, see the Visit Guernsey events diary for details.

Our top 12 days out in Guernsey are as follows:

Day One - Herm

As previously mentioned, a day trip to Herm is a must when visiting Guernsey. The ferries run frequently in the summer months and if you get a sunny day, the trip will remain in your mind for years to come.

Try and get a seat on the upper deck, so you can take in the marine traffic around St Peter Port, the views of the Islands all around you and of course the sun and sea air. The same location on the return visit will give you exceptional views of Guernsey, St Peter Port and Castle Cornet.

Don't forget sun cream and your camera. You can enjoy a meal while on the Island and you can shop for beach essentials in the small shops next to the harbour.

For something extra special you can enjoy a stay in the White House Hotel or hire self-catering accommodation. There is also a campsite which is very popular with the Guernsey locals. You can find out more on www.herm.com

Shell Beach - Herm

Day Two - The Little Chapel

This is reputed to be one of the smallest Chapels in the world. Decorated with shells and broken pottery this Chapel was the life's work of one Monk who lived in the adjoining former monastery, now the home of Blanchelande school.

In recent years a major refurbishment has taken place. A noticeboard next to the bus stop by the Chapel explains the history of the building.

Little Chapel, Guernsey

Once you have completed your visit, you could make the short journey to visit Bruce Russell, Gold and Silversmith at Le Gron, near the airport.

Entrance to the Farmhouse Hotel

If you prefer somewhere different you are also close to the Farmhouse Hotel where you can enjoy an excellent bar lunch or evening meal.

Day Three – A Sea Adventure around the coast.

Starting from St Peter Port, you can take an Island Rib voyage to the other Islands or along the base of the Island's South Coast Cliffs in one of their fast ribs.

It is a stunning adventure and something you will never forget. The tours operate from Easter until October Half term. Full details can be found about these tours on their website at: www.islandribvoyages.com

Photo Courtesy of Island Rib Voyages

If you like fishing, you can book a place on a local fishing boat and enjoy some "on the water" experience while hopefully catching some fish. Check out www.boatfishing.net

Day Four - Cliff Walking

The Coastal Cliff paths on Guernsey run from St Peter Port all the way to Pleinmont on the Islands Southwest corner. If you walked every path, you would walk almost 30 miles, as the paths zig zag and double back on themselves.

The direct run from St Peter Port to Pleinmont would see you cross a tarmac road in just a couple of places.

The views are generally amazing with a few exceptional vantage points giving you 'never to forget' photographic opportunities. Walking the entire length is a daunting prospect and is not recommended but there are three walks we really love to do.

For walk number one you park your car at Corbiere and walk to Le Gouffre for lunch (please book in advance as you don't want to walk there and find it is fully booked. Tel 01481 264121), before walking back to help burn off those calories. There are some quite steep elements in this walk so it is not for people who have walking difficulties.

My personal favourite is walk number two Fort George to Fermain Bay for a meal or just an ice-cream, this walk has wonderful views towards the other islands. Park your car by the German Military Cemetery and take the path south and down into the woods. There you will find signs on granite blocks which will point you towards Fermain. Again, this can be quite a steep walk, especially on the way back, so is not for the faint hearted.

The Cliffs above Fermain Bay

This walk will take you through the Bluebell woods, an extra bonus in the spring.

Finally, option three is drive to Pleinmont Point and take a walk past the German Fortifications – see below - down to the Imperial Hotel for a meal or a pint, remember it will be all uphill on the way back.

The cliffs can be muddy following wet weather so good walking boots or shoes are a must in those conditions. All have steep sections so if you are not a good walker stick to the upper paths to avoid the steeper sections.

Pleinmont restored Gun Battery

Day Five - Le Guet

Situated on the highest point along the Island's West Coast, the watch house at Le Guet overlooks the stunning bay at Cobo. In this part of Guernsey, the rocks of the coast turn to a golden brown as opposed to the usual grey.

This, along with the often turquoise sea and sandy bay, make the view from this vantage point worth the journey.

The small fort is fascinating, having been used by various defenders for many centuries. The pine forest which surrounds the fortification is also quite unique in Guernsey and despite appearances is a recent addition to the area.

Old prints of this area show the watch house standing out above the surrounding area. In the 2nd World War, the German Occupiers built fortifications into the hill which must have had uninterrupted views of the horizon.

If you visit during the evening, watch out for the ghostly figure of a German soldier patrolling the viewing area still looking out to sea for signs of an invasion or a passing ship.

Le Guet from Cobo Bay

Day Six - The Occupation Museums

Since the 2nd World War, several museums containing artifacts from the Occupation, have sprung up, some in the actual fortifications themselves.

Probably the oldest of these is the Guernsey Occupation Museum near the Airport. This provides an interesting insight into life during the Occupation.

Others include a museum at Havelet Bay, which occupies the site of some massive fuel tanks which were hidden in the hillside. These were probably used to fuel U-Boats. The German Underground Hospital doesn't have many exhibits but is a powerful demonstration of German life underground and how they used slave labour to create these huge structures.

On certain dates you can also visit a restored bunker at Vazon to see how the troops lived and if you are fit, you can climb to the top of one of the watch towers at Pleinmont. This climb, however, is by runged ladders and not for anyone who isn't physically fit and able to climb a ladder.

The Pleinmont headland is particularly well fortified and there you can see a recently excavated trench-work and coastal battery, with a large gun in place. Again, at certain times of the year, enactments are held, and the gun is fired.

Another must visit is the German Naval HQ next to the Collenette Hotel in St Peter Port. This bunker has been partly restored and features a film show which includes interviews with one of the German officers who worked in the bunker during the war.

It is a fascinating insight into the life of the troops who occupied the Island and shows how the bunker was utilized during the war years.

Underground Hospital

Day Seven - L'Eree / Lihou Island.

The land around the Lihou Island Headland has been designated a Ramsar site. The area includes the large shingle bank which protects the low-lying wetland which is known locally as the L'Eree Aerodrome.

This was where planes landed before the current airport was built prior to the 2nd World War.

The area of beach, in front of the shingle bank, is also protected and is a popular spot for bird watchers.

Nature Reserve at L'Eree

A good viewing point is near the entrance to the large dolmen in the area, near the tower in the above photograph.

If you can find the small rough car park on the hill next to the dolmen and in the shadow of the large German watchtower you can then walk around to the entrance and take in the view.

The Dolmen is what is known as a passage grave and is called locally Le Creux es Faies, when you pop in to look around don't forget to look out for the fairies!

If you walk or drive down to the L'Eree Headland
Car Park you will be able to look across to Lihou Island. This
small Island is connected to Guernsey at low tide by a
causeway but when the tide comes in it is cut off. If you are
planning a visit to Lihou be aware of the tides. A notice board
by the start of the causeway should give you up to date tidal
information.

You should be aware that there are no toilet facilities
on the Island and the lone house is only used for part of the
year.

One last thing to look at in this area is the memorial
to the poor souls that died on the MV Prosperity when she
ran aground on a reef near Lihou Island on the 16th of
January 1974.

It is a reminder of the many vessels and the hundreds
of lives that have been lost in the treacherous seas around
these Islands.

Day Eight - Castle Cornet and other Guernsey Museums

Castle Cornet has guarded the entrance to St Peter Port for over 800 years and is the flagship attraction of the Guernsey Museums service. In recent years they have offered a special entrance ticket which will allow you to get into the Castle, the Candie Museum and Fort Grey during your stay on the Island. If museums are on your "must do" list while you are in Guernsey this is a must buy ticket.

Castle Cornet, St Peter Port, Guernsey

During the summer, many re-enactments are carried out in the Castle and in some of the other historical locations like Fort Grey. This living history tells the story of Guernsey in an easy to understand and fun way.

The Guernsey Information Centre will have details of what is going on during your stay as will the events page on the Visit Guernsey website.

Other places to visit include the Martello (Loophole) Tower at Rousse which has fortified defence works, including replica cannons.

An explanation of how the Islands Martello or Loophole Towers to give them their correct name, were networked around the North of the Island to provide an overlapping defensive system is housed in the small stone building below the Tower.

Each Loophole tower had a similar associated building. These housed the gunpowder and munitions for the guns and soldiers who manned each tower.

Entry is free during the summer season, but the tower may be locked in the winter.

Many of the Islands defences have explanatory boards which describe the origins of the defences and how they formed part of the Islands overall defensive strategy.

Martello (Loophole) Tower at L'Ancresse.

Day Nine - A Walking Tour of St Peter Port

Particularly during the summer, there are many organised walking tours of St Peter Port. These are carried out by accredited guides and take in the long and often colourful history of this amazing town.

One we had great fun on, was an evening Ghost walk through the back streets of the town. This culminated with a nice meal in one of the town's fine restaurants, to help us warm up from the chill of the night and the chill of the many "haunting" stories.

Details of the various walks on offer and the starting times and meeting points can be found in the Guernsey Information Centre.

I have also produced my own self-guided walking tour of the seafront, from the ferry terminal to Castle Cornet. You will need a set of headphones to listen to my dulcet tones. The tour can be found at –

voicemap.me/tour/guernsey

St Peter Port, Guernsey.

Day Ten - Go Karting family fun Day Out.

Track Lane, near the boundary between the parishes of St Peter Port and St Sampsons, on the Island's east coast has long been a popular sporting venue on Guernsey. Home, until recent years, of the Island's premier football stadium, it also hosts a go karting track which runs around the perimeter of the pitch.

Many go karting events are held here during the year but when official races aren't being held you can hire a kart and have a go yourself. This is a popular way for families to compete against each other and as a way for many to get their first experience of single-seat motor racing.

Alongside "The Track" was the MFA Guernsey Bowl. Unfortunately, this closed down in 2017 and there is no indication that the facility will open again.

You can find out more about Go-Karting in Guernsey at:

www.kartingguernsey.co.uk

If you want to visit another attraction before or after your go-karting experience, a trip to Oatlands Village, a short drive away, is worth a visit. You can eat there and as previously mentioned there are some brand new attractions on site. There is a crazy golf course and several things for young children to do as well as a range of shops, including Craftwise for all your crafters, and of course the original brick kilns.

There are dozens of alternatives if you like different types of sport, many of which are mentioned in this Handbook.

The Brick Kilns at Oatlands

Day Eleven - Victor Hugo's House Tour

Open from April to September, Victor Hugo's House in Guernsey is well worth a visit. Victor Hugo is arguably Guernsey's most famous resident of all time. He spent most of his 19 years in exile from France in Guernsey and wrote most of his famous book Les Miserables while living in his home in St Peter Port.

To get a flavour of what you can see in this amazing house have a look at their website at www.victorhugo.gg

Tours of the house are held at certain times of the day so please contact the house or the Guernsey Information Centre before planning your visit.

You are unlikely to get a space on a tour if you just pitch up, but you can normally get access to the gardens at the rear of the house. There are plans to turn the Tourist Information Centre into the Victor Hugo Centre.

Currently this is only a conceptual idea, but if funding can be found, this is what they hope to achieve. www.vhc.gg

Day Twelve - Trip to Sark

Last, but certainly by no means least, is a visit to the fourth largest of the Channel Islands. Sark has its own website (www.sark.info) which explains all about the Island, how to get there and what to do while you are there.

There are no cars on Sark, which means to get around you will need to either walk, bicycle, take a tractor ride or enjoy a horse drawn carriage tour of the Island.

Welcome message on the tunnel at Maseline Harbour, Sark

There is much to see, some delightful hotels if you fancy a longer stay, and some good food to be enjoyed.

Sark has such an interesting story to tell, worth a book of its own, especially the story of the occupation of the Island during the Second World War. As a place to visit, it is great if you like beautiful views, peace and tranquility. It is also listed as a special dark sky location for the budding astronomers amongst you.

If you are looking for something more active then this may not be for you, unless you like sheep racing! (see the Sark Events Diary)

There is more on how to get to Sark later in the book.

Eating Out

Guernsey is blessed with many wonderful restaurants offering a range of different cuisines including English, French, Italian, Indian, Thai and Chinese; plus, many more.

If you want a take-away there are several options for Pizzas, Chinese, Indian, Thai and English food. You can also enjoy a fish and chip meal from several excellent chippies around the Island. Beetons and the Cobo Fish and Chip shop being at the top of our list.

Cobo Chip Shop, right next to the beach

Several restaurants have excellent reputations and are well supported by the locals – always a good sign.

To help you make the most of your time we have listed our favourite restaurants at the end of the Guide. The list is in no particular order but during recent years we have seen a few new restaurants join the list, most notable being Otto, a lovely new Italian restaurant on the northern outskirts of St Peter Port and Fifty-Seven, on the seafront on the heart of town.

Al Fresco on the Terrace at Moore's Hotel

You should note that smoking is banned in all enclosed public spaces, such as Restaurants, Bars and Clubs.

This means you should enjoy your meal without worrying about smoke. However, if you like a smoke with your meal, you may find a few places where you can enjoy a meal outside, weather permitting.

It looks like we eat out a lot!!

The last on this list is part of a group of restaurants which we like to frequent as they have an excellent loyalty scheme called the Inndulgence Club. To see the full list of their restaurants in Guernsey and Jersey and their current menus have a look at www.liberationgroup.com

A couple of newer restaurants include the Slaughterhouse and Octopus which are excellent locations for everything from a casual drink to a wonderful a la carte experience, Octopus has excellent views over Havelet Bay to Castle Cornet while the Slaughterhouse has a small outside terrace with views back across Havelet Bay towards Octopus.

(**Addendum**: It is worth noting that at the beginning of 2024, Octopus was ravaged by fire and is currently closed. I am not sure whether the owners will be able to rebuild in time for the 2024 season, but we wish them well and hope it will be back in full operation soon.)

The inside of the Slaughterhouse still has reminders of its original use – I'll say no more in case you are vegetarian.

Octopus, with Castle Cornet in the background

Staying in town there is a small Italian called Gusto near the top of Smith Street and for something different you can always try Balthazar, a steak and seafood restaurant.

Another excellent restaurant experience is Buho, a Mexican themed restaurant. In the same building they have the Escape Rooms. They can provide an exciting experience if you can find your way out.

Don't forget in the summer during seafront Sundays, many of the restaurants on the seafront go 'al fresco' and set up their tables in the road outside their premises.

These are enjoyed by locals and visitors alike and even the cruise passengers sometimes stop and enjoy an impromptu lunch in the sunshine to watch the world go by.

Indian Meal Al Fresco on a Seafront Sunday

Beach Kiosks

It would be remiss of me if I failed to mention the wide range of beach kiosks and cafes that are located all around the Island. Almost every beach has a kiosk of some kind where you can find anything from Ice-creams to full blown meals.

Starting in St Peter Port, one of our favourite places is the small kiosk by the Model Yacht Pond. There you can enjoy a tea or coffee and a range of foodstuffs and sweets in a beautiful location right next to Castle Cornet. You can sit by the kiosk or walk across to the Harbour where you can sit and watch all the boats coming and going through the harbour mouth. It is a lovely spot.

In the summer an ice cream van will be parked at the top of Havelet slipway, serving delicious whippy style ice-creams as well as a range of the usual ice-lollies.

Going clockwise around the Island is an impressive café next to the bathing pools, that has just been rebuilt. At Fermain Bay there is a lovely café where you can get hot food as well as drinks and ices. Jerbourg headland has a nice kiosk next to some public toilets alongside the car park. There you can sit and look out at the other Islands or, if you are feeling energetic, you can take a walk down to the bottom of the cliffs. It is a long way down and even longer on the way up.

Next is the Kiosk at Saints Bay and then another larger kiosk at Petit Bot. There was a kiosk at Icart Headland, but I believe that is now closed. There is nothing else along the cliffs until you reach Pleinmont. Down at the bottom end of Rocquaine Bay there is a nice kiosk with outdoor seating. Great for anyone who decides to take the walk out to the Star Fort or Fairy Ring at Pleinmont Point.

L'Eree Bay is usually served by an Ice Cream van but there is a café (currently closed as I type) opposite the toilets which used to serve all sorts of items and had some inside space for rainy days. Maybe it will open again this summer.

Next is the southern end of Vazon Bay which has a kiosk which is open pretty much all year round. Towards the North end of Vazon Bay is a larger café, called Vistas. It is located on the seaside of the road near Crabby Jacks. That has loads of inside seating, as well as roof top space. It serves substantial meals all year round. It is especially popular with bikers at the weekends.

Carrying on northwards the next kiosk is located at the south side of Cobo Bay. From there, if you look north, you can see the Grandes Rocques kiosk which is another popular location with the locals. They serve excellent winter warmer food outside of the summer months.

Carrying on around the coast one of the Islands larger kiosks is located at Port Soif Bay. If it is open, you will see the flag flying from the flagpole above the kiosk as you drive along the coast. It has a nice small sunken garden where you can enjoy your meal or an ice-cream.

Carrying on North you will find a popular kiosk at Rousse headland. Renowned for its cakes, this kiosk is in a lovely spot for anyone thinking of visiting the renovated Martello/Loophole Tower at Rousse.

Across the bay you could probably see the Ice-cream van based next to the playground at Les Amarreurs, if it is still in place, and further north the Kiosk at Chouet Bay. Not far from that is the Roc Salt Café/Restaurant which serves nice meals if you want to be indoors.

Before you get there at the end of Grande Havre bay there is a kiosk which is right next to a bird hide which looks out over the wetland known as the Vale Pond. Another popular spot with locals, you can get all types of food and drink there, pretty much all year round.

Then across the North of the island there is a small kiosk at Pembroke next to the bigger restaurant, with associated kiosk, called the Beach house. At the L'Ancresse Bay end of the northernmost beach is another kiosk. This one is rented out on a yearly basis as there was talk of it being knocked down. With works delayed I am pretty sure it will be open again in 2024.

The Beach House at Pembroke Bay

Bordeaux Bay offers another small kiosk called Woodies, popular with the locals and tradesmen looking for a coffee and maybe a bacon sandwich. Continuing your journey around the coast will bring you to St Sampsons Harbour where there is a small kiosk built into an old weighbridge called CJ's. It offers a range of takeaway food.

Occasionally I have seen an Ice Cream van at the north end of Belgrave Bay, but after that there are no more kiosks or mobile vans until you get back into town. Saying that there are a couple of places renowned for their bacon sandwiches and breakfasts.

There is a small sandwich shop at the Longstore which does excellent bacon rolls and when you get back to the harbour, you will find the most famous Café of them all, the White Rock Café on the North arm. There you might rub shoulders with politicians and fishermen, all putting the world to rights over a cup of tea and an excellent bacon roll.

Shopping

For most people, a visit to the shops and the buying of souvenirs are essential parts of a holiday. St Peter Port, the Island's capital, is where you will find most of the shops.

The High Street, Commercial Arcade and Pollet form the core shopping area. Extensions to this area to the South and West go up the Bordage, around the restored Market Buildings and on to the old quarter, which is home to a range of small quirky shops and cafes/restaurants. It is antique hunter heaven.

Some well-known names can be found in town, as it is known, such as M&S, Next, Boots, Mountain Warehouse, Schuh and Fatface. Amongst these are local shops selling a wide range of goods including perfumes, jewellery, technology goods, souvenirs, and clothing. There is no VAT in Guernsey, so prices should be competitive.

Town is the serious place to shop but out of town there are many hidden treasures for the serious shopper.

The Bridge, as it is known, is the second largest shopping centre on the Island, with a range of small shops serving the populous areas around St Sampsons and the Vale.

In recent years it has become a popular place for Charity shops but in amongst them are some jewellery and clothing outlets, which includes the Diamond Museum at Ray and Scott, one of the Island's top jewellers.

Out of these built-up areas you can find the Island's top jewellery outlet near the Airport. Bruce Russell is a world-renowned Goldsmith and his premises, which includes a restaurant and beautiful gardens, is definitely worth a visit. It is also worth searching for Catherine Best's jewellery workshop which is housed in an old mill to the south of town.

St Martins has a small shopping center with food and gift shops as well as local clothing and furniture stores and is also worth a visit. It is worth noting that most shops in town and in the other retail centres close on a Sunday.

The Island also boasts some impressive garden centres, which are open all week. Amongst these, Le Friquet Garden Centre stands out. It has a wide range of products above the usual plants and gardening paraphernalia, including clothes and household items. It also has a very nice tea-room and restaurant.

At Christmas it houses an Ice Rink and has a spectacular grotto area.

Earlswood, near L'Ancresse is another favourite and it too has a nice café which is very popular with the locals.

All shops accept English currency, and a few will accept Euros. Normal credit cards are usually accepted in all but the charity shops.

There are plenty of cash points in town and on the bridge.

Folklore

The Island of Guernsey is steeped in Folklore. Many books have been written on the subject over the years. If this is something that interests you, then I recommend purchasing Folklore of Guernsey by Marie de Garis.

One of the most obvious examples of Guernsey folklore are the witches' seats. These can be found on many of the older properties. They are stones that protrude from the walls, usually on the gables, where it is said witches could rest. By providing the seats you would keep in the witches' good books. Then they would not come into your house.

Witches' seats on the gable of a Guernsey house

Amongst the stories there are many mythical creatures. One of the more famous is the black dog of Cornet Street and Hauteville.

A lot of the stories relate to the full moon and are probably linked to smugglers and piracy. The full moon was a great time to carry out nefarious practices, so if you could scare people away during those times, you could do whatever you were doing without being discovered.

You can also see witches' marks on some old doors in St Peter Port. They look like pairs of spectacles, carved into the doors. The spectacles are shaped a little like an eight with a gap and a bridge between the two circles.

We have been on a nighttime guided walk around St Peter Port. We were told tales of ghosts and hauntings. It was a fascinating, if not slightly scary experience.

Tower Hill has a particularly sad story associated with its location. Three, so-called, witches, a mother and her two daughters, were burnt at the stake there, one giving birth while she was being consumed by the flames. Her baby was rescued but then thrown back into the flames by the Bailiff of the time. The poor boy was born and died on the same day, just because he was the child of a falsely convicted heretic.

A new book, covering the topic of Guernsey Folklore has been released in October of 2022. It is called Once Upon an Island, written by Penny Dawes. A new folklore trail has also been set up, in conjunction with the book, but at the time of writing I am not sure if this is permanent or just a temporary project.

As you know the Islands were occupied by the German Army under the orders of Hitler in 1940.

Many fortifications were built on the Island. Most used slave labour. Soldiers died during the occupation and slaves died because of the hardships they faced.

German Military Cemetery at Fort George

Stories abound of their ghosts walking around some of the fortifications or the sounds of digging being heard in some of the tunnels.

I have my own story to add to the list. I was driving up the Talbot Valley a few years ago when I was passed by a motorcycle and sidecar travelling at speed in the opposite direction. I was convinced it would hit me as it was on the wrong side of the road.

In the instant it flashed past me it seemed to pass through the wing of the front of the car. When I looked in the mirror it was gone.

It was only after that I realized it was a military vehicle and that the occupants had been two German soldiers. It still makes the hair on the back of my neck stand on end when I think about it.

One last thought. If you are passing the Longfrie Inn in St Saviours, look up towards the chimney on top of the gable facing the road. If you are lucky, you might see a witch looking down at you.

Guernsey's place in the World

Many people, when you mention Guernsey, have no idea of where we are, but for some reason seem to know the name. This is because the Island, though small, has had a huge impact globally. Suffice to say this small piece of land with just over 60,000 souls' punches well above its weight.

The word Guernsey has its own definition. A Guernsey is a woollen jumper worn originally by fishermen and over time was exported as far as Australia. There it became known as the kit worn by people who play Australian rules football. Though not made of waxed wool, the players still all wear Guernsey's.

The Guernsey Cow is also widespread with herds located around the globe, famed for the excellent quality of their milk. If you are travelling around the Island look out for the distinctive brown and white cattle.

Guernsey is still self-sufficient in local milk, and you won't find long-life milk on supermarket shelves. You will also find Guernsey cream in many shops.

The finance industry has also put Guernsey on the global map with people investing their monies and funds in the Island's well-run finance sector.

You will find Guernsey owned businesses in many locations. One of our most famous brands is Specsavers, which began business as a locally owned company. Before the Finance sector the Guernsey Tom was well known all over the UK as was the Guernsey Freesia, and we shouldn't forget the Guernsey Lily.

Then of course you have all the famous people who have their origins on this small isle. Sir Isaac Brock, the saviour of northern Canada was a Guernsey man. He is still celebrated in that country with Brock University named after him.

Admiral James de Sausmarez fought with Nelson at the Battle of the Nile and is renowned for his Victory in the Battle of Algeciras. He fought against the Dutch and then the Americans during their revolutionary war.

I've already mentioned his ancestral home which is situated in St Martins. Admiral James de Saumarez went on to command HMS Victory, after it was recommissioned following the Battle of Trafalgar.

These are just two examples of how Guernsey people have influenced our world. A quick search for Guernsey people on Wikipedia will provide you with a list of men and women who have done everything from winning VCs in the British army to contributing to the advancement of medical science.

Guernsey people have achieved sporting success, the Island producing world champions in several sports. The Island also produced a pioneer in the printing of bank notes and one trader introduced the UK to the delights of coffee from Costa Rica.

The world may well have been a different place without the many and varied contributions of the sons and daughters of our small Island. Look out for blue plaques and memorials to our people as you explore the Island during your visit.

Guernsey Cows happily grazing on a gorgeous day.

Getting Around

Whether you arrive by sea or air, you will need to get around the Island, starting with the trip to your hotel. Bearing in mind that the Island is only 24 square miles in size, nowhere is going to be very far away.

Taxis are usually waiting for you at the Airport and at the Harbour, though at peak times you may have to queue. You can avoid the wait by booking a taxi before you arrive. The driver will show you to your hotel, and if you engage him in conversation may even tell you what's happening while you are on the Island.

Be sure to pick up one of the Essential Guernsey Maps before you leave the Airport or Harbour Terminal.

Buses are also available from the Airport if you are just seeking a run into St Peter Port. If you fancy exploring by bus, we recommend you get yourself a bus timetable or download their app' as soon as you arrive and plan your days.

The coastal run can be fun and at certain times of the day will take you all the way around the Island.

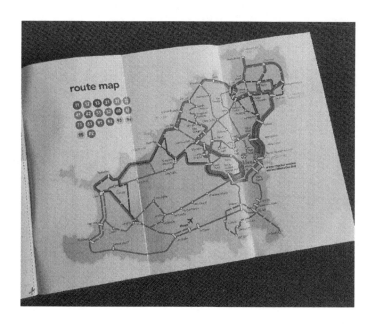

Bus Map included inside the Timetable.

However, the buses do not run late at night so if you are planning a bus trip and an evening meal, check out the timetable to be sure you can get back. All trips cost a flat rate of £1.50 (2023 rates). If you are planning to use the bus often during your stay you can buy a Puffin Pass which reduces your journey costs significantly (£1.00 in 2023).

This can reduce the cost of travel considerably. There are also several types of passes you can utilise to keep the cost of your journey down.

Make sure you get the up-to-date bus timetables and better still, visit the buses.gg website. There you will find a complete Guide to the local bus services. www.buses.gg.

On that website, you can also see their bus tracker which will tell you where your bus is in real time.

Buses at the Bus Terminus in St Peter Port

Bicycles can be hired if you are feeling fit and want to explore on two wheels. Electric bikes are also available which will take away some of the strain. However, the Island's roads are narrow so be careful if you are not totally confident on a bike. Cars and larger vehicles can get very close to you and there are precious few cycle tracks.

It is also illegal to cycle on the pavements, except along the front between St Sampsons and St Peter Port which has a cycle path on the pavement.

Scooters and motorbikes can be hired and can be a fun option but be careful on the narrow roads.

For many who come by sea, bringing the car with all the things you want and the capacity to take back all those souvenirs, is a great option. It is vitally important that as soon as you get off the boat you are aware of the differences between driving in Guernsey and elsewhere.

As with the UK, we drive on the left. The maximum speed limit is 35mph and in some built up areas, coastal areas and around schools, this can be reduced to 25mph or 20mph.

Diversions, due to road works, are frequent, so a good road map to help you find your way around is vital. Satnavs will work here and help you get around.

Road names are mostly in French, if you can find them, and directional signs tend to be general in content and few and far between. Many of the main tourist attractions are quite well signposted with the standard international brown signs.

This main thoroughfare into town is not always this quiet

There are a few roundabouts, but many locals are not very good with these, so be careful. However, the biggest factor to be aware of is the widely used "Filter in Turn" system.

These are signposted with an inverted triangle, stating "Filter in Turn" in advance of the junction, while the junction itself has a yellow hatch box junction painted on the road. The words Filter in Turn are also usually painted on the road on the approach to the junction.

The idea of these junctions is that traffic takes it in turns to cross, as it says on the sign, you filter, in turn. It is important to watch out for these junctions, particularly where traffic is fast moving, as a car coming from a side road on to the filter will have priority if they reach the junction before you. And of course don't go on to the hatched area if your exit isn't clear.

When travelling around you will see yellow arrows in the road. This isn't a one-way system, as many believe. These arrows warn you that a yellow line, a stop junction, is coming up – usually 25 yards away. Yellow lines along the side of the road mean no parking at any time; we don't have double yellow lines on the Island.

Parking is also different. Currently there is no charge for parking though changing to paid parking is always being considered. Currently there are no plans to introduce paid parking in 2024 that I am aware of.

In St Peter Port, and in many public car parks around the island, you will need to set a clock and be aware of the amount of time you can stay in the various disc zones.

By and large, the closer to the town centre, the less time you will have to park. Generally, the zones run for ½ hour, 1 hour, 2 hours, 3 hours, 5 hours and 10 hours. Large blue signs will tell you what is permitted. Some parking spaces are size restricted. There are Electric Parking points on the North Beach and parking zones for smaller cars.

Long term parking is at a premium in St Peter Port so if you are planning a trip to Herm for the day, be careful where you park, or perhaps get a bus or taxi into town for the day.

Parking clocks can be bought from the Guernsey Information Centre, the local Police Station in town or from many stores and garages around the Island. They cost a few pounds. Failure to set a clock properly or overstaying the amount of time permitted in the parking zone can result in a fine.

Obviously, the above applies to drivers whether they bring their own car or hire a car while on the Island. Hire cars are relatively cheap, so for a short stay they can be more cost effective. You should be given a parking clock and road advice when you collect the vehicle.

It is also worth noting that the price of petrol has risen quite a lot in recent years and is now more expensive than in the UK. On the plus side, a full tank is more than likely to last you a couple of weeks, unless you decide to drive around the Island until you get giddy!!

The Other Islands

Guernsey is blessed to be part of a group of Islands, all within easy reach of each other and all with their own unique character.

In order of proximity to Guernsey we will run through those that are accessible, all year round.

Lihou Island

Accessible on foot at low tide, Lihou Island is located off the Island's West Coast near L'Eree Bay. It has a ruined priory which has been the subject of extensive archaeological work over many years. There is a single building on the Island which is used as a Youth Hostel from time to time.

There is a warning about the tides at the start of the causeway and we recommend you read this carefully. On certain days you can walk across in the morning, enjoy being cut off during the day and having the Island almost to yourself and then walk back in the evening.

Lihou Island from the air

However, there are no toilet facilities on the Island, shops for refreshments or telephones.

From time to time there are walking tours of Lihou so look out for those.

A recent story of interest was the discovery of a range of unexploded shells on the Island. Apparently, the Germans used Lihou Island for target practice during the occupation!

Herm

Situated some three miles to the East of Guernsey, Herm is the main playground for the Islands boating fraternity and those that have fallen in love with this beautiful small Island. A short, 30-minute, boat ride from St Peter Port will take you to Herm Harbour or to Rosaire Steps, according to the tide.

The White House Hotel looks out towards Guernsey and is a lovely place to stay if you want to get away from it all. There are no cars on Herm and few roads. The few permanent residents either walk or rely on tractors or quad bikes for transport. There is also a camp site, and many Islanders enjoy a week or two there in the summer.

Fishermen's Beach in Herm

The Mermaid is the main bar for the Island, and they do excellent bar meals.

The new Herm Toilet Block next to the Mermaid Bar

Walking across the Island you will soon find yourself at Shell Beach or Belvoir Bay. Both beaches are amazing suntraps. A walk all the way around the Island is worth the effort and will give you great views of the other Islands in the Bailiwick.

For full details check out the Herm website at www.herm.com

Travel Tips and Links:

Trident Ferries offer regular trips to the Island starting at 8am from the 1st of April. You will be given a time when you must come back. Don't miss the boat. Adult fares in 2023 were £16.00 return for adults and £7.50 for children.

For up-to-date information on trips to Herm visit - http://www.traveltrident.com/

Sark

A much longer boat trip away (60 minutes), Sark is a different world and well worth a visit. You can enjoy a day trip to Sark, but it is so beautiful you may want to stay a bit longer.

The Island does have several excellent hotels and guest houses as well as a range of self-catering units. You can see the list of 2024 accommodation options on the www.sark.co.uk website.

The Town Centre in Sark! (Photo courtesy of J Moore)

Travel from Maseline Harbour to the top of the hill is either by foot or by the toast rack (see below), a tractor drawn trailer. This costs around £1.50 for adults and £1.00 for children.

When you arrive, if you are staying in Sark, your bags are automatically taken to your hotel, make sure your bags are labelled.

You walk through a tunnel to the waiting toast rack or if you are feeling very fit you can walk up the hill. Not for the faint hearted!

Once at the top of the hill, you can hire a bike, or a horse drawn carriage and explore this Island of tranquility.

The tunnel to Maseline Harbour in Sark.

The Island has a few shops and a good bar or two, if you feel the need to take a break and enjoy a drink.

The Seigneurie Gardens are worth a visit and while looking around the Island you will discover the strange laws that still rule this unique Island.

The way taxes are paid, and land is owned, is feudal in origin and the Seigneur has unique powers. Cars are forbidden on the Island, as is flying over the Island – the exception being visits by royalty.

Take a torch for walking around in the evenings as they have no street lighting.

As a result of those dark nights, Sark has special dark sky status making it a wonderful place for anyone interested in astronomy.

The view down from La Coupee.
(Photo courtesy of J Moore)

From Sark you can see Jersey clearly as well as the coast of France.

In 2016 we had the pleasure of visiting Sark for a family event. We stayed at the wonderful Stock's Hotel which was excellent with great food and friendly staff. I would highly recommend this Hotel to anyone looking for a bit of luxury when visiting Sark. We also ate at the restaurant in the Seigneurie Gardens and the food there was wonderful.

We took a Horse drawn carriage, that was an experience not to be missed, especially if, like me, you had never been in a horse drawn vehicle before.

Some of the roads and paths are basic, so good walking shoes are essential. The 'short cut' path down to Stocks Hotel was literally just a path alongside fields of sheep so we were pleased the weather was dry, especially when we came back from the event.

There is a Gold Bollard at the harbor, marking the achievement of Sark born John Guille in becoming a powerboat world champion in the UIM Class 3A World Offshore Powerboat Championships which were held in Guernsey in 2014. Also look out for the Gold Letter Box, which celebrates the gold medal that Sark born Carl Hester won in the 2012 Olympics.

For more information on Sark visit www.sark.co.uk

Travel Tips and Links:

The Isle of Sark Shipping Company offers regular sailings to
Sark. www.sarkshippingcompany.com
As regards finding somewhere to stay, we suggest you
visit:

www.sark.co.uk/where-to-stay/

Alderney

Travelling to Alderney is usually by plane but in recent years a ferry company has offered regular sailings to the Island. We took one of these trips last summer. It was great fun, but it was quite rough.

We sat at the back of the boat in the sun and were quite wet by the time we reached Alderney Harbour. You can book a trip using their website at http://www.alderneyferryservices.co.uk

The company operates a vessel called the Causeway Explorer and a one-way ticket will cost £54 for adults in 2024.

Aurigny fly there on a regular basis and landing there is a unique experience, particularly if you are only used to travelling in bigger planes.

Braye Beach, Alderney

The Island is the third largest of the Channel Islands and the most northerly. It has an amazing breakwater, which was built by the British to provide a safe anchorage for the British fleet.

For the ultimate in luxury stays, book a night at the Braye Beach Hotel. The photo above was taken from that hotel - www.brayebeach.com

Alderney has many good hotels and guest houses, a 9-hole golf course and some great pubs. It has blonde hedgehogs and just off the coast there is an amazing Gannet Colony at Les Etac. In fact, standing on the cliffs, watching and listening to the sounds of the colony is a wonderful experience.

The Gannet Colony off Alderney

The tides around Alderney can be extremely fast. I have watched a boat moving backwards because of the force of the current, so if you are sailing over yourself, take special note of the tides. You may save yourself a lot of time.

In the Second World War, the Alderney population was evacuated, and the Island was used as a concentration camp by the Germans.

The population wasn't allowed back until the 15th of December 1945, well after the war was over. That day is celebrated annually as Home Coming Day.

A sombre war memorial to the slave labourers who died during the occupation is a poignant reminder of those awful days.

The War Memorial in Alderney

Alderney must be one of the most heavily defended locations in the world with forts dotted around everywhere. It is now the place to be for on-line gambling companies with many of the big names holding licences to operate from the island.

It is arguably the only true Channel Island with all the others being in the Bay of St Malo.

Alderney week during August is their big festival but book your accommodation and travel early as the Island is very busy that week.

The Braye Beach Hotel, Alderney

Travel Tips and Links:

Air travel to Alderney is available all year round by Aurigny in one of their Dorniers. To make a booking visit www.aurigny.com

Alderney Ferry Services will be offering trips to Alderney in 2024. Keep a watch on their website at – http://www.alderneyferryservices.co.uk

Our favourite hotel in Alderney is the Braye Beach Hotel – see photo.   www.brayebeach.com

Jersey

If you are visiting Guernsey and have time to spare, a quick flight to the biggest of the Channel Islands is worth taking.

The West Coast of Jersey from La Moye with Guernsey in the distance.

The flight time by Blue Islands is about 10 minutes. If you do fly to Jersey, a great way to get to the town is to jump on the Number 15 bus to St Helier, which runs every 15 or 20 minutes from the airport terminal, depending on the day of the week you visit. It costs around £2.50 per person.

They operate double decker buses on this route, so you can get a splendid view of Jersey's south coast on your way into town. St Helier, the capital of Jersey, is more commercial than St Peter Port in Guernsey and the waterfront is getting quite built up, but it has a vibrancy all of its own and the town has a great range of shops to choose from.

Unlike Guernsey, they still have their traditional market, which is well worth a visit. On our last trip in December 2023, we enjoyed a delicious hot chocolate in the Market and on a previous visit we had a meal in Hugo's which is right opposite one of the main entrances to the Market.

Mum with Baby Gorilla in Jersey Zoo, December 2019

From St Helier you can get a bus to almost anywhere on the Island. The bus terminus is hidden right in the sea front area of town, close to the Pomme D'Or Hotel. Most people during a visit will head to the impressive Jersey Zoo, which we did in 2019, but there are many other attractions including the excellent Lavender Farm and of course Jersey Pottery.

The zoo was established by the late Gerald Durrell, and it specialises in conservation work. You can easily spend a day just looking around this beautiful zoo, taking particular note of the famous Gorillas and of course the Meerkats. In fact, you can find out more and even adopt a Jersey Meerkat at http://www.durrell.org/home/meerkat/

The zoo took a severe battering during storm Ciaran in 2023 but hopefully it will be fully up and running by the summer of 2024.

Like Guernsey, Jersey was also occupied during the second world war and to mark their liberation in 1945 a wonderful statue was installed in Liberation Square on the 50th anniversary – see photo.

Jersey Liberation Monument in St Helier

Jersey is also blessed with some fabulous Hotels and Restaurants so while you are there take in a meal in the shadow of Gorey Castle or sit outside at St Aubin and look out towards St Helier and Elizabeth Castle.

For Christmas, the Royal Square in the centre of town is converted into a winter wonderland for the annual Feté de Noué. When we visited there in 2023 there was music and entertainment, mulled wine and sausage baguettes, as well as a full range of local crafts, with a Christmas twist.

Outside the Royal Hotel was a French Market and a large Ice rink.

If you choose to stay at the Royal Yacht over the festive season and you are a light sleeper and like an early night, it may be better if you choose a room that doesn't look out over the event space. It can get quite lively.

During our short stay in December 2023, we stayed at the excellent Ommaroo Hotel in the Havre des Pas area just to the east of St Helier. There is a bus stop just outside and the Number One bus passes in each direction every 15 minutes during the week. In the opposite direction to St Helier it goes to Gorey, which is well worth a visit.

We also popped into the world-famous Jane James ceramics workshop in St Helier during our visit. With other artists in residence, I would highly recommend a visit if you are in St Helier. www.jane-james.com

Travel Tips and links:

You can travel to Jersey either by plane, using Blue Islands, see our travel links section, or by boat on Condor.

For more information about Jersey visit www.jersey.com

Our favourite hotels in Jersey are the Royal Yacht which is in St Helier., the Ommaroo in Havre des Pas, The Pomme D'Or or the Grand Hotel. For the best in terms of convenience, there is a Premier Inn in the heart of St Helier.

For a special treat visit just before Christmas and enjoy the Feté de Noué.

And Finally

When you start spending money on the Island you will be amazed to get your change in Guernsey's own currency. The Guernsey pound is equivalent to the UK pound, so you will have no exchange differences to worry about but whereas you can spend British pounds in Guernsey, you can't spend your Guernsey money in the UK.

You can spend Guernsey currency in any of the Channel Islands, but it isn't accepted in the UK. You will also find £1 notes in your change rather than £1 coins. The coins are legal tender in the Island but not well used. Many people take a £1 note back as a souvenir.

Guernsey coins are different too so make sure you check your change before you leave and try and change any Guernsey notes for English one's before you go home.

To conclude this book, we have listed below 2 web sites that we hope you will find useful if you want to carry out any further research into Guernsey before making your journey.

Guernsey Government Web Site:
www.gov.gg
Visit Guernsey Web Site:
www.visitguernsey.com
Useful Numbers:
Guernsey Police
Tel: 01481 725111
Beau Sejour Leisure Centre (Bookings)
Tel: 01481 747200
Princess Elizabeth Hospital (including A & E)
Tel: 01481 725241

There is a reciprocal medical agreement between Guernsey and the UK which means holiday makers from the UK who become ill while on the Island can access emergency and necessary healthcare for free while in the Bailiwick. For full details please visit - Reciprocal Health Arrangement - States of Guernsey (gov.gg)

Guernsey is a separate jurisdiction and has no National Health Service as there is in the UK. Guernsey people must pay when they visit the Doctor and Dentist, although there is a scheme which covers locals for any essential major treatment they might require.

We hope you enjoyed reading this Handbook and thank you for your purchase. If you find something you feel we have missed or could be changed, please let us know by emailing us at tonybrassell@gmail.com

The New Liberation Statue outside the Visitor Information Centre

The Author

This handbook has been compiled and written by Tony Brassell. He was born and raised on the Island and has lived there for almost all of his life. He spent a long career in the Civil Service, acquiring a wide knowledge of Guernsey and has a keen interest in the Island's heritage and culture, in a wide range of areas.

He spent many years acting as the Island's native guide, within the Civil Service, and has escorted VIPs at the highest level, including a Deputy Prime Minister, when they have visited Guernsey.

When he left the Civil Service, he established a local tour company called Experience Guernsey Limited and operated that business until 2008. From 2006 to December 2019, he worked as a Business Advisor with the Guernsey Enterprise Agency, trading as Startup Guernsey, and in 2020, he stood down from being the Branch Officer for the IoD Guernsey Branch after 7 years working with them.

He builds, hosts and maintains websites for businesses and private individuals as well as writing novels and painting in watercolour. You can see some of his work on www.tonybrassell.co.uk.

He was a single handicap golfer and in 2012 was Captain of the L'Ancresse Golf Club but had to retire from the sport due to back issues.

His unique perspective on Guernsey through a lifetime based on the Island, and years of promoting the Island, make him an ideal Author of this Handbook. He promised to give an honest appraisal of Guernsey, explaining what works and what doesn't.

Importantly if you are planning a stay on the Island, he believes that you should make the most of your time, seeing as much as you can, while still taking time to relax and enjoy the peace and quiet that is easily found on this beautiful British Channel Island.

Other books by Tony include:

Ten Days One Guernsey Summer, a story linked to the Evacuation of the Island in June 1940. This is available in local bookshops and on Amazon as a paperback or on Kindle.

Journey Home, a novella describing how two evacuees, one from Jersey and one from Guernsey find their way home to the Islands from Taunton at the end of the second world war.

The Battle for Guernsey, an alternative history novel, describing an imagined invasion of the Island by British troops as part of D-Day in the summer of 1940.

Project 75, the first science fiction novel in a series called the Warriors of Sol. More will follow.

A New Future, the second in my Science Fiction series.

The Kangaroo Ace, A fictional First World War story about a woman who became the only female flying ace of that conflict.

The Witches of Witherwack – River of Blood, the first in the DI Karen Dee series of Detective stories based in Sunderland.

Footsteps in the Sand, the second in the Witches of Witherwack series.

More books are currently underway including a third in my detective series and a third in my Science Fiction series.

Appendices

Hotels, not all of them.

Driftwood Inn	01481 264436
Cobo Bay Hotel	01481 257102
The OGH	01481 724921
Moores Hotel	01481 724452
Duke of Richmond	01481 726221
La Fregate	01481 724624
Havelet Hotel	01481 722199
St Pierre Park	01481 728282
Hougue Du Pommier	01481 256531
The Bella Luce	01481 238764
La Barbarie	01481 235217
Jerbourg Hotel	01481 238826
Les Douvres	01481 238731
Fermain Valley Hotel	01481 235666
Farmhouse Hotel	01481 264181
L'Auberge du Val	01481 263862
Imperial Hotel	01481 264044
La Trelade	01481 235454
La Villette	01481 235292
The Peninsula Hotel	01481 248400
Les Rocquettes	01481 722146
Saints Bay Hotel	01481 238888
Les Cotils	01481727793
Le Chene Hotel	01481 235566

NEW - Premier Inn Guernsey — Book online

Guest Houses

Charmaine Guest House	01481 245583
St George Guest House	01481 721027
Castaways Guest House	01481 239010
El Tabora Guest House	01481 721341
Grisnoir Guest House	01481 715458
Marton Guest House	01481 720971

Self-Catering Apartments

Vazon Bay	01481 254353
Adair Bungalows	01481 253991
La Barbarie Apartments	01481 235217
Rocquaine Bay	01481 254353
The Bay, Pembroke	01481 247573
Wisteria	01481 257113
L'Aumone House Barn	01481 256841
Albany Apartments	01481 712392

Visit www.visitguernsey.com for more details with regards to accommodation.

Restaurants

The Slaughterhouse	01481 712123
Otto	01481 710888
La Fregate Hotel	01481 724624
Pier 17	01481 720823
Good Rebel	01481 811591
Buho (Mexican)	01481 235666
Le Nautique	01481 721714
Mora's	01481 751053
Da Nellos	01481 721552
Cobo Bay Hotel	01481 257102
Hotel de Havelet	01481 722199
La Perla	01481 712127
Dhaka	01481 723692
Marina Restaurant	01481 247066
Beach House	01481 246494
Crabby Jacks	01481 257489
Christies	01481 726624
Village East	01481 700100
The Boathouse	01481 700061
Dix Neuf	01481 723455
Deerhound	01481 238585
Fleur du Jardin	01481 257996
Bella Luce	01481 238764
Imperial Hotel	01481 264044
Longfrie Inn	01481 263107
Terrace Tea Garden	01481 724478
Deerhound Inn	01481 238585
Pony Inn	01481 244374
Octopus	01481 722400
19 Bar and Grill	01481 740019
The Dragon Chinese	01481 244688
The Indian Cottage	01481 244820
The Kiln	01481 245661
Puffin and Oyster	01481 200141
Moore's Hotel	01481 724452
The Taj Indian	01481 724008
The Pickled Pig	01481 721431

Printed in Great Britain
by Amazon

43197598R00071